Polar Bears

Kate Riggs

CREATIVE EDUCATION
CREATIVE PAPERBACKS

seedlings

Published by Creative Education and Creative Paperbacks
P.O. Box 227, Mankato, Minnesota 56002
Creative Education and Creative Paperbacks are
imprints of The Creative Company
www.thecreativecompany.us

Design by Ellen Huber
Production by Chelsey Luther
Printed in the United States of America

Photographs by Corbis (Alaska Stock, Daniel J. Cox, Paul
Souders), Dreamstime (Outdoorsman, Igor Stevanovic,
Sergey Uryadnikov, Jiri Vaclavek), Getty Images (Grant
Faint), National Geographic Creative (BILL CURTSINGER,
WILD WONDERS OF EUROPE/LIODDEN/NATUREPL.COM),
Shutterstock (ILYA AKINSHIN, Sylvie Bouchard, Iakov
Filimonov, Eric Isselee, Vladimir Melnik, Nagel Photography)

Library of Congress Cataloging-in-Publication Data
Riggs, Kate.
Polar bears / Kate Riggs.
p. cm. — (Seedlings)
Summary: A kindergarten-level introduction to polar bears,
covering their growth process, behaviors, their Arctic home,
and such defining features as their all-white fur.
Includes index.
ISBN 978-1-60818-515-3 (hardcover)
ISBN 978-1-62832-115-9 (pbk)
1. Polar bear—Juvenile literature. I. Title. II. Series: Seedlings.

QL737.C27R548 2015
599.786—dc23   2013051258

CCSS: RI.K.1, 2, 3, 4, 5, 6, 7;
RI.1.1, 2, 3, 4, 5, 6, 7; RF.K.1, 3; RF.1.1

First Edition
9 8 7 6 5 4 3 2 1

TABLE OF CONTENTS

Hello, polar bears!

Polar bears are big bears.

They live in cold
and icy places.

Polar bears have thick fur. It is white, just like the snow and ice.

White polar bears have black noses. Polar bears use claws to walk on ice.

Polar bears
eat meat.

They hunt for seals
and walruses.

Baby polar bears are called cubs. Cubs live with their mother. Adults live alone.

Polar bears like to swim.

They watch
for seals to
pop out of
the water.

Goodbye, polar bears!

Picture a Polar Bear

ear

eye

snout

nose

teeth

fur

legs

paw

claw

21

Words to Know

claws: curved, pointed nails on the paw

fur: the short, hairy coat of an animal

walruses: ocean animals related to seals that have two long teeth called tusks

Read More

Schuetz, Kari. *Polar Bears*.
Minneapolis: Bellwether Media, 2012.

Turnbull, Stephanie. *Polar Bear*.
North Mankato, Minn.: Smart Apple Media, 2013.

Websites

Arctic Animals Coloring Pages
http://www.hellokids.com/r_1647/coloring-pages/animal
-coloring-pages/wild-animal-coloring-pages/arctic-animals
-coloring-pages
Print out pictures of polar bears to color.

Polar Cam
http://zoo.sandiegozoo.org/cams/polar-cam
Watch the polar bears at the San Diego Zoo.

Index